Bible reflections
for older people

BRF

15 The Chambers, Vineyard
Abingdon OX14 3FE
brf.org.uk

Bible Reading Fellowship is a charity (233280)
and company limited by guarantee (301324),
registered in England and Wales

ISBN 978 1 80039 136 9
All rights reserved

This edition © Bible Reading Fellowship 2022
Cover image © iStock.com/ArtMarie

Acknowledgements
Scripture quotations marked with the following abbreviations are taken from the version shown.
Where no abbreviation is given, the quotation is taken from the same version as the headline reference.
NIV: The Holy Bible, New International Version (Anglicised edition) copyright © 1979, 1984, 2011 by
Biblica. Used by permission of Hodder & Stoughton Publishers, a Hachette UK company. All rights
reserved. 'NIV' is a registered trademark of Biblica. UK trademark number 1448790. NLT: The Holy Bible,
New Living Translation, copyright © 1996, 2004, 2007, 2013. Used by permission of Tyndale House
Publishers, Inc., Carol Stream, Illinois 60188. All rights reserved. NRSV: The New Revised Standard
Version of the Bible, Anglicised edition, copyright © 1989, 1995 by the Division of Christian Education
of the National Council of the Churches of Christ in the United States of America. Used by permission.
All rights reserved.

Every effort has been made to trace and contact copyright owners for material used in this resource.
We apologise for any inadvertent omissions or errors, and would ask those concerned to contact us so
that full acknowledgement can be made in the future.

A catalogue record for this book is available from the British Library

Printed and bound in the UK by Zenith Media NP4 0DQ

Contents

About the writers

Ro Willoughby has been writing and editing Christian resources for many years. She has recently been licensed as a lay minister at St Chad's Woodseats in Sheffield, where she is engaged in ministry with people of all ages. She enjoys being closer to her children and grandchildren, as well as close to Bakewell and Chatsworth House!

Tony Horsfall is a freelance trainer and retreat leader based in Yorkshire. His BRF books include *Resilience in Life and Faith* (2019) cowritten with Debbie Hawker, *Servant Ministry* (2019, second edition), *Spiritual Growth in a Time of Change* (2016) and *Rhythms of Grace* (2012). He also contributes to BRF's Bible reading notes *New Daylight*.

Sally Rees is a retired nurse, priest and Anna Chaplain. She is the Anna Chaplain lead for Wales and the bishop's officer for older people's ministry in the Swansea and Brecon Diocese. This is her first contribution to *Bible Reflections for Older People*, after being involved with the Anna Chaplain carer's guides (**brfonline.org.uk/carers-guides**).

Angela Tilby worked for the BBC as a producer of religious programmes for 22 years. She also spent time in academic and parish ministy before moving to Oxford – first as diocesan canon of Christ Church Cathedral and now as canon emeritus. She writes for the *Church Times* and broadcasts frequently on Radio 4's *Thought for the Day*.

From the Editor

Welcome.

'Was she someone?' enquires the nurse, bustling around her frail, elderly patient as she 'heaves and tucks and smooths'.

The question rings through the opening scene of Penelope Lively's 1987 novel *Moon Tiger* and has stayed with me ever since I read it. The gravely ill, elderly woman in the hospital bed is a historian and former war correspondent with a colourful, turbulent past. The kindly but unseeing nurse speaks to her like a small child and addresses her question to the doctor. He consults his notes as they walk away. 'Yes,' he replies, 'the records do suggest she was someone, probably.'

Born in 1933, Penelope Lively has written numerous prize-winning novels and short story collections for both adults and children. In 2013 she published *Ammonites and Leaping Fish* which she describes as, 'not quite a memoir. Rather, it is the view from old age.' In her preface she writes of the 'very few people' who, after they've gone, 'are distilled into a blue plaque on a building.'

The famous blue plaque – one of the most tangible signs that someone was a 'Someone'. It's unlikely that any of us will ever be honoured with a blue plaque, but as each one of the writers in this issue affirms, in God's eyes we are all 'Someone'. Whatever our age, status or circumstances, each one of us is named, unique and infinitely precious in his sight.

God bless you.

Using these reflections

Perhaps you have always had a special time each day for reading the Bible and praying. But now, as you grow older, you are finding it more difficult to keep to a regular pattern or find it harder to concentrate. Or, maybe you've never done this before. Whatever your situation, these Bible reflections aim to help you take a few moments to read God's Word and pray whenever you have time or feel that would be helpful.

When to read them

You might use these Bible reflections in the morning or last thing at night, but they work at any time of day. There are 40 reflections here, grouped around four themes, by four different writers. Each one includes some verses from the Bible, a reflection to help you in your own thinking about God, and a prayer suggestion. The reflections aren't dated, so it doesn't matter if you don't want to read every day. The Bible verses are printed, but you might prefer to follow them in your own Bible.

How to read them

- **Take time** to quieten yourself, becoming aware of God's presence, asking him to speak to you through the Bible and the reflection.

- **Read** the Bible verses and the reflection:
  - What do you especially like or find helpful in these verses?
  - What might God be saying to you through this reading?
  - Is there something to pray about or thank God for?

- **Pray**. Each reflection includes a prayer suggestion. You might like to pray for yourself or take the opportunity to think about and pray for others.

Children matter

Ro Willoughby

How often have you heard an adult, when referring to their childhood, say, 'My dad (mum, grandmother, godmother, Sunday school teacher) really prayed for me. I'm so thankful'? They are so grateful for those who have nurtured their Christian faith. Sadly, fewer and fewer children have this experience today as Christian observance declines and Bible stories are increasingly unknown.

In this series we focus on the importance of children in the Bible. I hope this inspires us to pray for children and young people we know, for those who care for them and for children in need throughout the world.

Children have many wonderful opportunities. We thank God for that. But they are not shared equally. Young people's mental health and sense of identity have been impacted by the pandemic, by social media, by poverty and by broken relationships. In many countries children are caught up in war zones, live in refugee camps, are poorly fed and educationally deprived. We cry to God on their behalf and give thanks for those who have nurtured our own faith.

2 Chronicles 34:1–21 (NIV, abridged)

A boy king reigns

Josiah was eight years old when he became king… In the eighth year of his reign, while he was still young, he began to seek the God of his father David. [Ten years later] Hilkiah the high priest found the Book of the Law of the Lord that had been given through Moses… When the king heard the words of the Law, he tore his robes… 'Go and inquire of the Lord for me.'

Many people have had a difficult childhood which affects them for the rest of their life. Josiah had a bad start. His grandfather, Manasseh, was unfaithful to God. His father, Amon, was just as bad, reigned for just two years and was murdered in his palace. Yet Josiah 'did what was right in the eyes of the Lord' (v. 2).

We're not told who was responsible for Josiah's upbringing, but the godly Hilkiah, the high priest, features strongly in the story of Josiah's reign. Idols of false gods were destroyed, the dilapidated temple was repaired, the book of the law was read aloud and the people turned back to God.

Whether or not you came to faith as a child, thank God for those in your childhood who showed you, by their words, actions and example, what it meant to belong to Christ.

■ PRAYER

Pray for any parents, family members and youth workers you know, who are committed to nurturing Christian faith in young people. So many things can drown out the life-saving news of Jesus.

Luke 1:64, 68, 76 (NIV, abridged)

A father sings

Immediately [Zechariah's] mouth was opened and his tongue set free, and he began to speak… 'Praise be to the Lord, the God of Israel, because he has come to his people and redeemed them… And you, my child, will be called a prophet of the Most High; for you will go before the Lord to prepare the way for him.'

Zechariah and Elizabeth longed for a child. At that time being childless was shameful, often seen as a sign of God's punishment. No wonder Zechariah was stunned when the angel Gabriel told him not only that he was going to have a son called John, but that this son would prepare the way for the coming of the Messiah. He was struck dumb because he did not believe the angel's words. He remained dumb until the boy was named and circumcised, eight days after his birth. Immediately, words of praise to God poured out from Zechariah. His tongue was 'set free'.

Zechariah had two reasons to rejoice – the time had come for God to rescue his people and, at last, he had become the father of a boy who, amazingly, mattered to God.

■ PRAYER

All children matter to God. All are known to God. Pray for Christian parents to see their children as God's gift to them. He has a purpose for them from the day of their birth. Pray for parents to do all they can to enable their children to know Jesus for themselves.

Luke 2:16–19 (NIV)

A mother wonders

[The shepherds] hurried off and found Mary and Joseph, and the baby, who was lying in the manger. When they had seen him, they spread the word concerning what had been told them about this child, and all who heard it were amazed at what the shepherds said to them. But Mary treasured up all these things and pondered them in her heart.

Most mothers cannot take their eyes off their newborn baby. They wrap tiny little fingers around their forefinger. They stroke a peach-soft cheek. Mary was no different from any other mother. But she had even more to wonder – and to fear. In many senses, her son was an ordinary boy. We assume he had a normal childhood, the village carpenter's son, the eldest child in the family.

But he was also most extraordinary. Angels had announced his miraculous conception and birth. Wise men from the east had called by with exotic gifts. Mary was warned that a sword would pierce her heart. As a family they became refugees. Her son was God become man.

Charles Wesley, the hymn-writer, wrote these words: 'Our God, contracted to a span, incomprehensibly made man.' We should never forget just how extraordinary it was that God, in the form of Jesus, should take on human flesh to become a child. Like Mary, we can treasure this up in our hearts.

■ **PRAYER**

Talk with God about what it means to you that he understands the joy and frailty of humanity, of being a child.

Luke 18:15–17 (NLT)

Children welcomed

One day some parents brought their little children to Jesus so he could touch and bless them. But when the disciples saw this, they scolded the parents for bothering him. Then Jesus called for the children and said to the disciples, 'Let the children come to me. Don't stop them! For the Kingdom of God belongs to those who are like these children. I tell you the truth, anyone who doesn't receive the Kingdom of God like a child will never enter it.'

'Why do trains go into tunnels? How does this torch work? Where does snow come from?' Some young children are forever asking questions. Their curiosity equips them to make sense of life. What is more, they experience the world in all its freshness which fills them with awe and wonder. Their vulnerability invites them to be trusting and calls for adults to care for them.

The curiosity of adults can get blunted. We can become overfamiliar. We can lose our sense of wonder. Our experience may make us less trusting of others. This means our relationship with God can become dull and boring. Jesus, however, calls his disciples, indeed all people, to come to him as a child – to trust him, to question him wanting to know more, to be overawed and yet welcomed into his kingdom.

■ **PRAYER**

As a child, what fascinated you about God's world? Can you remember a time when you could trust God in a childlike way? Ask Jesus to make you curious to know him more deeply, delight in him more joyfully and trust him more simply.

Luke 7:12–15 (NIV)

A mother mourns

As [Jesus] approached the town gate, a dead person was being carried out – the only son of his mother, and she was a widow. And a large crowd from the town was with her. When the Lord saw her, his heart went out to her and he said, 'Don't cry.' Then he went up and touched the bier they were carrying him on, and the bearers stood still. He said, 'Young man, I say to you, get up!' The dead man sat up and began to talk, and Jesus gave him back to his mother.

Luke injects lots of detailed emotion into this short story, one of only three times when Jesus brings someone back to life. It almost seems as though Jesus comes across the funeral procession by chance. But there is nothing random about Jesus' reaction. He acts decisively. The son's death probably meant his mother had lost any means of support. She was both sorrowful and destitute. It is beautiful to read that Jesus touched the coffin (which would have made him ritually unclean), spoke to the boy, then lovingly restored him to his mother.

Imagine yourself walking towards Jesus, holding close to you any sorrow, challenge, disappointment or fear you are experiencing at the moment. Jesus can see your sadness and his heart overflows with compassion. He may not take the grief away as he did so dramatically in this story, but he understands and he cares – and that makes all the difference.

■ PRAYER

Pray for anyone you know who is currently grieving. Pray also for parents who are struggling to support their own children.

Matthew 15:22–28 (NLT, abridged)

A mother pleads

A Gentile woman who lived there came to [Jesus], pleading, 'Have mercy on me, O Lord, Son of David! For my daughter is possessed by a demon that torments her severely'... [Jesus'] disciples urged him to send her away. 'Tell her to go away'... Jesus said to the woman, 'I was sent only to help God's lost sheep – the people of Israel.' But she came and worshipped him, pleading again, 'Lord, help me!'... 'Dear woman,' Jesus said to her, 'your faith is great'... And her daughter was instantly healed.

As a woman and a Gentile foreigner (not a Jew and therefore an outsider), this desperate, determined woman would never normally speak to a Jewish teacher like Jesus. That is why Jesus' disciples try to prevent her speaking to him. She demonstrates profound and bold insights into who Jesus is. She recognises he has the power to heal her daughter.

From the beginning Jesus made it radically clear that he had come to save the whole world, both Jews and Gentiles. Few people could grasp such a claim even after Jesus' death and resurrection – but this woman believed it. Her faith is remarkable, and Jesus acknowledges this with great tenderness.

■ PRAYER

We can ask Jesus for anything, trusting that he is all-powerful, all-knowing and all-caring. Pray for any parents you know who are desperate for someone to help their child in some way. Pray especially for parents who are refugees, living as foreigners in a strange land, whose children are traumatised and disadvantaged. Lord, help them.

Matthew 11:25–26 (NIV)

Like a child

At that time Jesus said, 'I praise you, Father, Lord of heaven and earth, because you have hidden these things from the wise and learned, and revealed them to little children. Yes, Father, for this is what you were pleased to do.'

I went to Sunday school in the afternoon. I sang choruses, sat still to listen to the story, put my hand up if I knew the answer to a question and maybe coloured a picture to take home. Children's groups in churches are very different now – and rightly so. Children are encouraged to ask questions, there is discussion and discovery and there is much more activity. What is more, adults leading the group expect to learn *from* the children. It is a two-way process.

Just before Jesus spoke to his Father, he had criticised the Jewish leaders for mocking John the Baptist and Jesus himself. For all their apparent wisdom, they had seriously failed to recognise John as the one preparing the way for Jesus, the Messiah. Jesus reminds his hearers that God makes himself known to those childlike in faith and trust.

God revealed himself through the prophets, through creation and through his wonderful deeds – but 'in these last days he has spoken to us by his Son' (Hebrews 1:2).

■ PRAYER

The best way to know God is to see him through Jesus, to be childlike in our faith and trust. Talk with God about how childlike you are in your relationship with him.

Matthew 21:15–16 (NIV)

Children shout loudly

When the chief priests and the teachers of the law saw the wonderful things [Jesus] did and the children shouting in the temple courts, 'Hosanna to the Son of David,' they were indignant. 'Do you hear what these children are saying?' they asked him. 'Yes,' replied Jesus, 'have you never read, "From the lips of children and infants you, Lord, have called forth your praise"?'

How often have you walked past a primary school at lunchtime, with children racing around in the playground? It appears joyously chaotic, although some ball games look more organised. If you look closely, an occasional child might seem isolated. Most noticeable, however, are the soundwaves of children's high-pitched voices.

Whole families travelled to the city of Jerusalem to celebrate the Passover. To their surprise Jesus rode into the city on a donkey. The crowds, including children, excitedly welcomed him. Some children then spilled into the temple courts to continue their joyful messianic cry, 'Hosanna to the Son of David!' That's what children do. Jesus neither silenced nor corrected them. Why should he? They were declaring what is true. By quoting Psalm 8 Jesus acknowledged the significant capacity of children to worship God.

■ PRAYER

Give thanks to God for the spontaneous and exuberant way children praise him, praying that they will never be silenced nor reproved. Ask God to make this nation's children resilient as they learn to live after the disruption of the Covid pandemic. May they discover God's great love for them.

Deuteronomy 10:17–19 (NLT)

Orphans and widows

For the Lord your God is the God of Gods and Lord of lords. He is the great God, the mighty and awesome God, who shows no partiality... He ensures that orphans and widows receive justice. He shows love to the foreigners living among you and gives them food and clothing. So you, too, must show love to foreigners, for you yourselves were once foreigners in the land of Egypt.

'Orphans and widows' is an umbrella phrase used to describe the needy in Bible times. Life was precarious. Disease was ever-present. Accidents happened. Local skirmishes resulted in violent deaths. Women died in childbirth and children died in infancy. Widows had to fend for themselves as best they could. Foreigners were always vulnerable.

The Old Testament law in Deuteronomy recognised the existence of the vulnerable in society and their need to be valued. God cared for those in need. His people were not to forget that they too had been outsiders in Egypt and in desperate need. We too are called to remember our experiences of God's care and provision, and to care for those in need throughout the world.

■ **PRAYER**

Pray for anyone you know who needs support and those who are seeking to support them. Pray especially for the children in need in war-torn countries, whose education has been interrupted, who have witnessed terrible sights, who may be bereaved and are hungry. Their childhood experiences will impact them for life.

Psalm 78:2–7 (NIV, abridged)

Adults to children

I will open my mouth… [and speak] things our ancestors have told us… We will tell the next generation the praiseworthy deeds of the Lord, his power and the wonders he has done… so that the next generation would know them, even the children yet to be born, and they in turn would tell their children. Then they would put their trust in God.

Families share their stories from the past. These days we have so many more means of preserving family memories, not just a few well-worn photographs and precious keepsakes. Electronically we save films of significant occasions and holidays, record the spoken voice or the performed song, store thousands upon thousands of photographs. We can trace our family history over several generations. The tales told may become fragmented or distorted. They may be delighted in or neglected.

More than anything the psalmist wants God's people to remember him and all the marvellous deeds he has done over the centuries. He has been faithful, compassionate, just, powerful, ever-present and… we could go on and on. These stories are not just to be remembered and shared among the adults. They are to be told to the younger generation so that they will come to trust in God for themselves.

■ PRAYER

Thank God for any group of Christians you know who are telling the stories of God's goodness to children and young people. May they do this with imagination, enthusiasm and truth.

From heaven you came

Tony Horsfall

If Paul had a favourite church, it would have been the one at Philippi. The exciting story of how it came into being is told in Acts 16. Among its members might have been Lydia, the businesswoman; the jailer and his family; and the young slave girl delivered from evil spirits. When he writes to the church in Philippi, Paul describes this congregation as his joy and crown (Philippians 4:1) and prays for their growth in grace with joy and thanksgiving (Philippians 1:3–6).

However, something was troubling the apostle, and his concern for the unity of the church is what prompted this letter. He had heard there had been a falling out between two of the most prominent leaders, and he writes to address this matter. He appeals to them all to be united despite their differences. To encourage them in this direction he points them to the example of Christ and the humble way he came into the world. You see, humility is the key to unity, and a servant heart the foundation of life together in the church, which is why these reflections focus on that particular message, explained in Philippians 2:1–11.

Most churches could do with taking Paul's message to heart. Unity will only be achieved if each of us is willing to walk in humility, just as Christ did.

Philippians 2:1–2 (NIV)

What we have in common

Therefore if you have any encouragement from being united with Christ, if any comfort from his love, if any common sharing in the Spirit, if any tenderness and compassion, then make my joy complete by being like-minded, having the same love, being one in spirit and of one mind.

The church I belong to is like a bag of liquorice allsorts. We are a disparate bunch of people who probably would not be together were it not for our common faith in Jesus. But then most churches are like that, aren't they? This is the wonder of the church – that God takes all kinds of people, who might not normally get on well together, and forms them into a loving family.

Paul begins by reminding his friends of the things they have in common, the truths that unite them. They have all experienced Christ's love, received his Spirit to live within them and known his merciful welcome in their time of need. This common experience of grace should bind them together, creating a beautiful spiritual oneness between them.

How is your church doing? How might you be an example of the approach that Paul is advocating here? What is your attitude to those who are different to you?

■ **PRAYER**

Lord, help me to see others, not through the lens of difference, but through our oneness in Christ. Amen

Philippians 2:1–2 (NIV)

Becoming like-minded

Therefore if you have any encouragement from being united with Christ, if any comfort from his love, if any common sharing in the Spirit, if any tenderness and compassion, then make my joy complete by being like-minded, having the same love, being one in spirit and of one mind.

Having reminded the Philippians of what they have in common, Paul now exhorts them to be like-minded, to develop a similar attitude and outlook based on their love for one another.

This does not mean they need to agree on everything or develop a rigid conformity of thought that robs them of their individuality. He is not calling for everyone to hold the same opinions. As we shall see as we read further, he is calling for us to be like Jesus in our thinking, for us to adopt his attitude when it comes to relating to one another. When each of us is focused on approaching others as Christ did, then we will be like-minded – sharing the mind of Christ.

How have your thoughts and attitudes towards others changed since you came to faith? Is there someone whom you find difficult, whom God wants you to see through his eyes?

■ PRAYER

Lord, may I not hold my opinions so tightly that they separate me from others. Help me to know the flexibility of the mind of Christ. Amen

Philippians 2:3a; James 3:13–14 (NIV)

The root of so much trouble

Do nothing out of selfish ambition or vain conceit... Who is wise and understanding among you? Let them show it by their good life, by deeds done in the humility that comes from wisdom. But if you harbour bitter envy and selfish ambition in your hearts, do not boast about it or deny the truth.

I have only recently taken up gardening, but I have discovered a surprising enemy – the humble blackberry. Its tendrils spread everywhere, and it quickly roots itself into the soil, making it hard to eradicate from my flower beds. When I trace these extensions back to their source, I find there is a knotted ball of roots that stubbornly refuses to be removed.

Pride, the root of most sin, is like that. In church, pride can express itself through the desire for position and power (selfish ambition) or in being opinionated, feeling superior and always needing to be right (self-conceit). These sinful attitudes ruin churches and break up whole communities if left unchecked.

It is good to pause sometimes for self-examination and ask God to show us our own hearts. Are these attitudes found in me? Have I unwittingly given room in my heart to bitterness?

■ PRAYER

Lord, help me to ruthlessly eliminate any attitude in me that might jeopardise the unity of your church or spoil my friendships. Amen

Philippians 2:3b–4, 20–21 (NIV)

The secret of good relationships

Rather, in humility value others above yourselves, not looking to your own interests but each of you to the interests of others... I have no one else like [Timothy], who will show genuine concern for your welfare. For everyone looks out for their own interests, not those of Jesus Christ.

Some people simply stand out from the crowd, don't they? Not always for their gifts or abilities but sometimes because of who they are – their character and personal qualities. The young man Timothy was like that, and he is the one to whom Paul is referring here.

What stood out about Timothy was his selflessness, his ability to put the needs of others before his own. Such a quality is a mark of a true servant, and it shows how the mind of Christ was at work in him.

If pride is the root of so much division and nastiness in church, humility is the source of harmony and well-being. The ability to step outside of one's own concerns in order to think about the needs of others is a mark of emotional and spiritual maturity. Those who are self-centred and inward-looking are immature and childish; they have not yet grown up spiritually.

■ **PRAYER**

Lord, help me to mature in Christ and be other-focused when necessary. Release me from a preoccupation with myself. Amen

Philippians 2:5; John 13:34–35 (NIV)

Christ our example

In your relationships with one another, have the same mindset as Christ Jesus… A new command I give you: love one another. As I have loved you, so you must love one another. By this everyone will know that you are my disciples, if you love one another.

A cartoon character makes this flippant remark: 'I love humankind… it's people I can't stand.' Perhaps you have felt that way sometimes. I know I have. Relationships can be a tricky business, and that is true even in church.

Paul is writing to the church in Philippi to encourage them to take care of their relationships. Some notable members had fallen out, and this breakdown in relationships was affecting everybody. He writes, 'I plead with Euodia and I plead with Syntyche to be of the same mind in the Lord' (4:2).

For relationships to work we must not only love one another, but also cultivate a humble mind, to develop an attitude like that of Jesus who was gentle and lowly in heart (Matthew 11:29). When we are proud and full of our own opinions, refusing to listen to others, we are more likely to find ourselves at odds with them. Those who are highly opinionated and inflexible seem to attract disputes like iron to a magnet. Fractured relationships, however, are not a good advert for the church.

■ PRAYER

Lord, teach me to be humble-minded and considerate of others. Amen

Philippians 2:6; 2 Corinthians 8:9 (NIV)

At home in heaven

[Christ Jesus], being in very nature God, did not consider equality with God something to be used to his own advantage... For you know the grace of our Lord Jesus Christ, that though he was rich, yet for your sake he became poor, so that you through his poverty might become rich.

Most people want to be upwardly mobile; that is, they want to climb the ladder of success. They aspire to live in a large house, be considered well off, and have status and recognition. Not so the Lord Jesus. He was downwardly mobile, exchanging the glory and privilege of heaven for the grim reality of life on earth and death on a cross.

Notice that, as the Son of God, Jesus was equal to the Father, sharing his divinity. In heaven he was worshipped and adored, revered by the angels for who he was. That was his rightful place, but he did not cling to either position or privilege. In order to save us he laid aside his glory so that he could enter our world. This downward descent shows his humble attitude; it reveals his mindset.

The willingness to walk the way of humility and lowliness of heart is a very Christlike quality, which, with God's help, we should and can emulate.

■ PRAYER

Lord, help me not to fear letting go of status and position. Grant me to be content wherever you place me. Amen

Philippians 2:7; Mark 10:45 (NIV)

Stepping down

Rather [Christ] made himself nothing by taking the very nature of a servant, being made in human likeness… For even the Son of Man did not come to be served, but to serve, and to give his life as a ransom for many.

In October 2021 a remarkable love story was played out in Japan before the world's media. Princess Mako, 30, the eldest daughter of Crown Prince Fumihito and niece of reigning Emperor Naruhito, tied the knot with university sweetheart Kei Komuro, a commoner, in Tokyo after an eight-year engagement. But it meant that she had to relinquish her royal position, let go of her family ties and be divested of all related privileges. What a sacrifice for the sake of love.

Such a stepping down from privilege and status to become a commoner is nothing compared to the way of self-emptying love demonstrated in the coming of Christ into our world. Through the incarnation Christ was born as a human being, but not to some exalted earthly position as we might expect. Rather he was born into humble circumstances and took upon himself not only human likeness, with all its limitations, but also the attitude of a servant.

Such love should fill us with wonder and amazement, and not only cause us to worship him, but also seek to be like him.

■ **PRAYER**
Lord, grant me a servant heart that finds joy in serving others. Amen

Philippians 2:8; John 10:17–18 (NIV, abridged)

Destined for the cross

And being found in appearance as a man, [Christ] humbled himself by becoming obedient to death – even death on a cross!... The reason my Father loves me is that I lay down my life... No one takes it from me, but I lay it down of my own accord.

Finding one's destiny and fulfilling one's potential are watchwords of our society. Young people are encouraged to dream their dreams of stardom and fame and believe that anything is possible for them. I'm not so sure of the validity of such an approach. What I do know is that such a philosophy is in stark contrast to the way of Jesus.

Jesus left the glory of heaven; he took human form; and now we see that he was even willing to suffer death and the ignominy of the cross. This was his destiny, a path of suffering foreordained for him, and one which he embraced willingly and in obedience to his Father's will. He stepped into our world to become the suffering servant.

We too are called to take up our cross and follow him, to deny ourselves in order to embrace the Father's perfect will for our lives (Mark 8:34). Discipleship means that we are to die daily to our own ambitions, choosing to follow in the footsteps of the one who walked to Calvary.

■ **PRAYER**

Lord, grant me courage to obey you and follow you wherever you lead me. Amen

Philippians 2:9–10; Hebrews 1:3b (NIV)

Risen and exalted

Therefore God exalted him to the highest place and gave him a name that is above every name, that at the name of Jesus every knee should bow, in heaven and on earth and under the earth... After he had provided purification for sins, he sat down at the right hand of the Majesty in heaven.

During World War II a fierce air battle was fought in the skies over Kent. British planes triumphed because they gained greater altitude than the enemy and could attack them from above. In such warfare, altitude determines victory.

Having followed Paul's description of the humiliation of Jesus in his descent from heaven to the depths of the grave, we are reminded that he did not stay dead. Rather, he was raised to life again and restored to his rightful place at God's right hand. Now the name of Jesus is the name of authority and power, greater than any other name we could think of.

When we pray in his name we operate from his heavenly altitude and bring his victory to bear on our own life and circumstances. We can triumph because he already has. When we feel defeated or overwhelmed, we can remind ourselves that Christ has overcome all opposition. He can help us because he has already conquered Satan and dealt with our sin.

■ **PRAYER**

Lord, remind me constantly that in Christ we have the victory. Amen

Philippians 2:11; Acts 2:36 (NIV)

He is Lord

And every tongue acknowledge that Jesus Christ is Lord, to the glory of God the Father... Therefore let all Israel be assured of this: God has made this Jesus, whom you crucified, both Lord and Messiah.

The greatest declaration we can make as believers is to say sincerely, 'Jesus is Lord.' When we make this confession, we are expressing our conviction that Jesus has been raised from the dead and is now seated at the Father's side. We are proclaiming that Satan is defeated and sin has been dealt with. We are saying that Jesus has been given ultimate authority.

When I say for myself, 'Jesus is Lord,' what I am actually saying is: 'Jesus is my Lord, and my life is lived in submission to him.' The more we allow him to control and direct our lives, the more we will live in harmony with each other. If I am submitted to Christ, and you are also submitting yourself to him, we are more likely to live in agreement. Our mutual acceptance of the lordship of Christ holds us together and helps create unity between us. In this way the prayer of Jesus that we may be one is made a reality (John 17:21).

■ PRAYER

Lord, may we fix our eyes on you, risen and exalted. May we willingly submit to your authority in the church and pursue unity with one another. Amen

The Gift of Years

 Debbie Thrower is the pioneer of BRF's Anna Chaplaincy for Older People ministry, offering spiritual care to older people, and is widely involved in training and advocacy.

Visit **annachaplaincy.org.uk** to find out more.

Debbie writes...

Welcome! Following in Shakespeare's footsteps, psychologist Erik Erikson identified seven stages of life – the middle years being ones of industry, identity and intimacy. However, after the age of 65 he felt – because of society's increasing longevity – that he'd begun to outlive his own categories! Hence, he added an eighth category of 'integrity': a time for seeing how a life contributes to the whole.

All the writers in this issue show how Christian faith informs a life's journey, especially in the later years. Each contributor is witnessing – in their unique way – to the fact that the righteous person is like a tree planted by living water, whose leaves stay green (Jeremiah 17:8).

These words remind me of another author, Emilie Griffin, who thinks 'adaptation' and 'transcendence' best sum up her own maturing: 'My focus is on a person's quest to live deeply and well,' she writes. 'My delight has been to raise good questions. Does later life have meaning?... What about lifelong learning? What is a good fundamental attitude about change and diminishment?'*

I hope these reflections, bursting with a fresh vitality, will help you to answer such good questions in your own *inimitable* way.

Best wishes

Debbie

* *Green Leaves for Later Years* (Intervarsity Press, 2012).

Meet Sally Rees

Retired nurse and nurse lecturer Sally Rees has been a key figure in the development of Anna Chaplaincy and is the Anna Chaplaincy lead for Wales. She was ordained in the Church in Wales in 2014 with a remit to develop older people's ministry across her ministry area: a large geographical area in South Powys and Blaenau Gwent consisting of ten churches, five care homes and two retirement housing complexes. She is now Anna Chaplain to this ministry area and continues to build teams of pastoral visitors around each of these places of worship and types of housing, equipping local Christians to provide spiritual care to those in need in their communities. She writes:

In 2005 our church set up a pastoral visiting team and I was asked to help coordinate it. Soon it became clear that the majority of those in need of pastoral visiting in our locality were people who were older in years, who were less mobile and beginning to become more dependent than they wished to be. This is when the need for a distinctive ministry with older people became clear to me.

After retirement, when I was exploring my calling to what God had in store for me next, I visited Debbie Thrower in Alton and shadowed her for a day. The day was varied, starting with a service of Communion with the Mothers' Union group, coffee and chat, and then visiting people with differing needs in their own homes and in care homes in Alton. It was amazing. I loved it. I found ministry with older people completely fulfilling and soon became convinced that this was the ministry for me. Debbie and I have been in touch ever since. I have been part of the Anna Chaplaincy network from the very first 'gathering' and have been privileged to witness Anna Chaplaincy and its ministry to older people in the community grow throughout the country.

During the last couple of years and with more than one lockdown, ministry in person has been very difficult. There have been many challenges, but ministry by phone, writing cards, leaving gifts of encouragement on doorsteps and distanced visits in gardens and through windows has continued. It hasn't been the same, or as satisfactory, for any of us, but a different and essential ministry has been offered. For some, it has been a vital lifeline.

In recent months one-to-one visits in person slowly resumed in individual homes, retirement housing and care homes, but with caution. Masks, social distancing and other precautions such as lateral flow testing prior to visiting became the norm. In our care homes we have been able to offer some services but with restrictions, such as being allowed no more than two non-residents to be present. Many homes have been open to visitors and then closed again, depending on shifting Covid regulations, so the kind of ministry we can offer continues to be uncertain from week to week.

I am still concerned for those in hospital, those who live on their own and those who are living with dementia, and their carers. Without being able to gather together and without opportunities to share conversations over tea and cake, I worry that some in need are being missed.

But looking on the brighter side, church-wide opportunities to gather for worship, meet for prayer, for meetings and social occasions on Zoom have blossomed for those who are able to use new technologies. Zoom has also opened opportunities to develop and engage in online learning. During this troubled period when going out has been limited, the Anna Chaplaincy network has continued to grow. The message of Anna Chaplaincy and the need to care for the spiritual needs of older people is gathering interest across the country. The number of people undertaking Anna Chaplaincy training online is growing all the time. I have run four of these training courses with people from across Wales and from different denominations who are beginning to plan how they might reach older people in their communities with the appointment of an Anna Chaplain.

It seems that God is always at work, in whatever circumstances we find ourselves in. While I have not been able to visit as many people in person, I have been using some of my teaching and writing skills from my time as a lecturer to help develop the ministry to older people for which I have such a passion. It makes me realise anew that God does not waste any of our life experiences. This is something I've often seen in older people's extraordinary lives but now, after these strange two years, I see it in my own life and in my own journey with God.

A King's colours

Glynda Winterson

Glynda Winterson introduces the second of her poems to feature in *Bible Reflections for Older People*.

In traditional representations Mary, the mother of Jesus, is usually wearing the colour blue. This was due to a well-intentioned desire to honour her because in the ancient world blue and purple dye were so rare and expensive that they were the colours worn only by royalty.

But while these pictures may be beautiful, I admit to sometimes feeling impatient with those artists and movie directors who have offered their viewers an unrealistic or tidied-up version of the characters, circumstances and events in the Jesus story.

In this poem I have tried to dispel the other-worldly image so often presented to us. Mary lived in the real flesh-and-blood world as we all must. She was called to trust God even when, travelling to Bethlehem while heavily pregnant, he did not seem to be arranging events to make her calling an easy one.

Sometimes we wonder why God has allowed particular difficulties to arise in our own lives. To be able to identify with someone who was as special as Mary and yet had to face life in all its gritty and sometimes grim reality can help to strengthen our own faith and trust in God. Let us not allow the pretty but unrealistic pictures to hide the very real human being who inspired them.

Copies of Glynda's collection *Making Light* can be bought from the poet for £7.00 including postage. Contact enquiries@brf.org.uk or call 01865 319700 and your request will be passed on.

A King's colours

Amazed by our visions
of a dry swept-clean stable

of a shy mother kneeling
in cloudless sky coloured silk
(white hands idly clasped)
she might say

no one from Nazareth
could afford the blues
of lords and kings

and laugh remembering
wet straw on an innkeeper's floor,
the baby's sick on the undyed
sheep's wool of her shawl

and her fingers still sore
red-raw from harvest,
from millstone, from cutting
the kindling for cooking,
from distaff and spindle and loom

or she might say nothing, no words
for the wonder and worry
interwoven over the years:

how from the hems and seams
of new tunics for a growing son

she would look up and watch him
at home with her in his earth colours.

From *Making Light* by Glynda Winterson,
used with kind permission.

Don't sideline ministry to older congregations – Joan Wager

Joan Wager is a member of Langwathby Methodist Church in Cumbria and a former circuit steward. An experienced spiritual director, she worked for 20 years in the probation service and in church and development work with The Children's Society. She believes profoundly that every Christian has a vocation, no matter what their age.

Why is ministry with older congregations seen in such a negative way? Or at least, it has increasingly seemed this way to me in recent years. I know of many church congregations where attenders are predominantly 'senior' – that doesn't mean they are inactive or 'passengers', and yet, invariably, when considering the mission of the church, leaders seem to focus only on the young.

I have begun to ask the question, 'Does God not call people to minister to older congregations or communities?' I have asked this informally, in church and circuit meetings, in a Zoom session about vocation and in a conversation about 'tired churches'. And the responses? Among the blank or slightly horrified expressions, the following stand out:

> 'I have one small church where they are all over 70, so I have to tell them what to do!'

> 'Older people in churches could worship by Zoom if they wanted to – they say they can't and want to get back to meeting together – but they are just wilful – they could do it if they tried.'

I wonder if ministry to older people is often neglected because ministers are faced with the demands and expectations about age profiles, pressures for church growth and the often expressed view that 'young people are the future of the church'.

I have been in so many church meetings where the question, 'What is your vision for the church ten years from now?' has been asked. I know of people who have been asked the same question at least four times over the years and have never seen any outcome from the exercise!

I believe there are other vitally important questions we should be asking: questions about the life-long journey of faith – the 'Always learning' that Angela Tilby writes about in these pages – about the church in the community, about social isolation. These questions are relevant to all age groups but are particularly relevant to older adults.

Has the church stopped listening? Has the church lost interest in our experience, our gifts and our vision as well as our vulnerabilities? We are told we must 'tell people about Jesus', but what about *listening* to people's stories? I fear we're losing the art of listening.

Yet maybe there is hope.

When I read in a report* on the implications of an ageing population for the church that 'the church has the chance to be a trail blazer', I was immediately hooked. Moreover, Kofi Annan, when he was secretary-general of the United Nations, challenged societies to address the experience of ageing populations, including their spiritual needs, and it is encouraging to see this is now beginning to happen, particularly within the church context. Some churches are appointing clergy or lay workers for older people, the growing network of Anna Chaplains offers spiritual care in later life and other models are emerging. The UN's annual International Day of Older Persons on 1 October is important symbolically and, hopefully, practically too.

There is still considerable scope to develop a ministry which recognises the needs of older congregations but, importantly, also recognises their gifts and wisdom. This is a challenge, but it is also a wonderful opportunity to build vibrant, intergenerational churches and communities that will flourish in the 21st century.

* by the organisation formerly known as Care Home Friends.

Surviving grief

Sally Rees

Sadly, we all know that the years living through the pandemic were particularly difficult for those who experienced the death of a loved one while isolated. Few of us were not touched in some way by the loss of someone close.

Everyone's grief journey is unique, of course, but ultimately I believe there is the hope that we can move forward; that it is possible to both honour our loved one's past and weave our memories of them into a new and hopeful reality. This may be almost impossible to believe in the depths of grief, but we can take heart, for God is with us and journeys with us as we adjust to loss and look to new beginnings.

When I was reading the Old Testament book of Ruth following the death of my mum in January 2021, I was amazed at how relevant, rich and raw this story of the women's experience of grief still is today. I found it of great help and I hope that you might find it helpful too.

Ruth 1:3–5 (NIV)

Devastating times

Now Elimelek, Naomi's husband, died, and she was left with her two sons. They married Moabite women, one named Orpah and the other Ruth. After they had lived there about ten years, both Mahlon and Kilion also died, and Naomi was left without her two sons and her husband.

When a spouse, partner, family member or friend dies, the grief that follows is often both disorientating and devastating. This was the case for Naomi, Orpah and Ruth. They lost their husbands, their status in society, income and perhaps even their home. They had no children so there was no prospect of anyone else looking after them.

The book of Ruth is amazingly relevant to us today, both in its realistic portrayal of grief and in highlighting the possibility of getting through it. Naomi, Ruth and Orpah were real people experiencing loss and joined in grief. They fear they have lost everything – a natural feeling when engulfed by grief – but God has a plan to help them get through these terrible times; they simply don't know this yet. Their story reminds us that God is with us and that there is always hope. Even when times are really bleak, God will provide.

■ **PRAYER**

Heavenly Father, we thank you that you are always with us whether we can feel your presence or not. Help, comfort and protect us as we cry out to you in the pain of loss and bereavement. Amen

Ruth 1:6 (NIV)

Difficult decisions

When Naomi heard in Moab that the Lord had come to the aid of his people by providing food for them, she and her daughters-in-law prepared to return home from there.

Without her husband and her sons, Naomi is left with the responsibility of providing for herself and her two daughters-in-law. She is faced with a difficult choice and decides to return with Ruth and Orpah to Judah, where she has heard that God has provided food for her people.

For anyone suffering bereavement, the weight of making decisions on their own can add an almost unbearable burden. It's not only lonely and sad, it is hard, really hard – but decisions are often also unavoidable in the midst of grief.

For those who are grieving, it can really help to have someone to talk through decisions and offer a clear, more objective perspective. The text doesn't say this, but I like to think that Orpah and Ruth will have listened to Naomi as she weighed her decision, giving her confidence that she made the right one.

■ PRAYER

Heavenly Father, thank you that you never leave us in times of trouble. We ask that you will send others to comfort, help and be present with us when difficult decisions need to be made. Amen

Ruth 1:8 (NIV)

Showing kindness

Then Naomi said to her two daughters-in-law, 'Go back, each of you, to your mother's home. May the Lord show you kindness as you have shown to your dead husbands and to me.'

In the midst of her sadness and grief, Naomi is still able to think of others. She thinks of Orpah and Ruth and considers their feelings, their prospects and their long-term futures. She wants what's best for them. Although Naomi's grief is great, in her care and thought for Ruth and Orpah, she shows tenderness and grace even though this will leave her on her own.

She not only gives them her blessing to leave her, but she also asks God to bless them too. Naomi has not lost her faith and has not lost her perspective on how life goes on for others. She wishes them well and asks God to look after them. Grief can sometimes harden our hearts and make us bitter, but Naomi shows that it is quite possible, even in bereavement, both to be very sad for yourself and to show deep kindness to others.

■ **PRAYER**

Heavenly Father, thank you for your love and care. When we are grieving and sad, save us from bitterness and hardness of heart. Help us to accept the love and care of friends, and at the same time, show kindness and compassion to others. Amen

Ruth 1:9–11, 14 (NIV, abridged)

Respecting others

Then [Naomi] kissed them goodbye and they wept aloud and said to her, 'We will go back with you to your people.' But Naomi said 'Return home, my daughters. Why would you come with me?'... Then Orpah kissed her mother-in-law goodbye.

What is so touching about these three people is their love for each other. Emotional and spiritual bonds can be close with family and friends, and grief has the potential to strengthen them. For these three, their experiences of life, love and loss have forged very strong connections and deep attachment. Parting is difficult. There is much weeping and Orpah decides to go back to her own people. There is nothing wrong with her decision.

Sometimes people who are grieving find it difficult to accept the reactions and decisions of close family and friends, but experience tells me that it's important to respect and support those decisions, even if you're shocked or disappointed by them.

Often there are no easy answers, nor a clear right-or-wrong path to take, but accepting others' decisions with grace, love and blessing can be healing. It can also help to preserve the strong bonds of shared history and experience.

■ **PRAYER**

Heavenly Father, help us to be generous-hearted to others, even when their decisions might affect us adversely. Help us, instead, to trust you to provide all that we need. Amen

Ruth 1:13b–14a (NIV)

Bitterness

'It is more bitter for me than for you, because the Lord's hand has turned against me!' At this they wept aloud again.

In the middle of her good wishes, Naomi cries out in pain and bitterness. When we are grieving, our emotions can change very easily and, as we saw earlier, sometimes our thoughts and feelings turn bitter and harsh. Suddenly, Naomi's feelings of loss overwhelm her; she becomes full of self-pity and blames God for her plight.

This is quite a 'normal' reaction to grief. Naomi feels her grief is different from everyone else's (which it is) and her anguish is focused on herself. The danger is that, in time, such a focus can become self-destructive.

When grieving, it is healthy to cry out to God. Almost a third of the psalms are laments where David is telling God exactly what he is feeling. Our heavenly Father knows our thoughts and hearts, so nothing surprises him. As our Father he wants to hear the cries of his children. Crying out to God is far better than shutting God out of our lives. And God always hears us and comes to our rescue.

■ PRAYER

Father God, when things look bleak and life has not turned out as we had hoped, help us not to become bitter. Instead, help us to turn to you, cry out to you and know your presence and healing through Jesus, our Lord. Amen

Ruth 1:16 (NIV)

Faith in action

But Ruth replied, 'Don't urge me to leave you or to turn back from you. Where you go I will go, and where you will stay I will stay. Your people will be my people and your God my God.'

This is surely the most well-known verse of Ruth and the key verse of 'her' story. Despite all the uncertainty that may follow, Ruth chooses to stay with Naomi, to be with her and care for her. Why?

Ruth has not only grown in love and respect for her mother-in-law, but she has also found faith in Naomi's God, the God of Judah. She does not want to leave either Naomi or her faith behind. She decides to step out in faith with Naomi and utters those intensely moving words: 'Your people will be my people and your God my God.'

Despite her difficulties, Naomi has clung on to her faith in the God of her fathers and Ruth has seen the impact. It is wonderful to know that even in circumstances where we might feel completely helpless, God is not only with us but can use us to further his kingdom. God uses weak and broken people to bring glory to himself.

■ PRAYER
Heavenly Father, help us in our weakness to know that, whatever our circumstances, you are with us and will bring good out of our lives, for your glory. Amen

Ruth 1:22 (NIV)

Acceptance

So Naomi returned from Moab accompanied by Ruth the Moabite, her daughter-in-law, arriving in Bethlehem as the barley harvest was beginning.

This verse marks a pivotal place in these two widows' bereavement journeys.

Maybe this is Naomi's lowest point, but she has arrived home in more ways than one. She is physically home with Ruth, but she has also come to a place where she seems to have accepted her situation. In grieving there are usually lots of ups and downs, but for most people there comes a time of acceptance of life without the loved one. Naomi's return home has perhaps reinforced this. Acceptance of loss and forging a new kind of life without the loved one is hard, but it is healthy. Ten years have passed since Naomi left home. Acceptance can take some time.

They arrive in Bethlehem as the barley harvest is beginning, spring-time: a time and symbol of new life, hope and provision. From the depths of the darkness of grief, there is light and hope for the future. Like the barley seeds that have been hiding in the dark of the earth, new life is emerging.

■ **PRAYER**

Thank you, Father, that you can lift us out of the darkness of grief and give us your light and hope for the future. Amen

Ruth 2:3 (NIV)

God-incidences

So [Ruth] went out, entered a field and began to glean behind the harvesters. As it turned out, she was working in a field belonging to Boaz, who was from the clan of Elimelek.

In this verse the words 'as it turned out' are seemingly just thrown in, although there is no coincidence here. Why are we so surprised that Ruth 'finds herself' working in a field belonging to Boaz, a close relative?

God had these two widows in his care and he is good. We, of course, also have the benefit of knowing the end of the story. Ruth finding herself in this field is what some people like to call a God-incidence. Although she was willing to work hard, God had guided her to a safe place, a place where she could look forward to a different kind of future. I wonder what she and Naomi had been praying.

Sometimes it is easier to look back to see clearly where God has had his hand on our lives and acknowledge the God-incidences, but just like Ruth and Naomi, we can trust in God's love, care and provision.

■ PRAYER

Heavenly Father, we thank you for your love and care for us, sometimes in hidden blessings. Thank you for walking alongside us, guiding us and keeping us safe. Amen

Ruth 2:20 (NIV)

God's provision

'The Lord bless [Boaz]!' Naomi said to her daughter-in-law. 'He has not stopped showing his kindness to the living and the dead.' She added, 'That man is our close relative; he is one of our guardian-redeemers.'

Enter the guardian-redeemer. Almost halfway through the book of Ruth we find out that the person God has placed before Ruth and Naomi is someone who can redeem their situation.

I wonder if you remember Green Shield Stamps. You could 'redeem' those stamps to 'buy back' the value of really amazing things, usually household goods. Here, at the end of Ruth 2, we find out that Boaz is able to re-establish the family line, the line lost through the death of Ruth and Orpah's husbands, Mahlon and Kilion. He is able to restore them back into society and security. He can protect and provide, and honour the past and the present. He is also able to play a part in the future. How wonderful.

There are parallels here to remember about the one who saves us, redeems our past, keeps us secure and promises to be with us into the future until we meet him in heaven – our Lord Jesus Christ.

■ PRAYER

Heavenly Father, thank you for this beautiful story reminding us of the amazing God that you are and for your Son Jesus Christ who redeems the past, present and future. For us as individuals and for the world, we give you our thanks and praise today. Amen

Ruth 4:9–10, 13, 17, 22 (NIV, abridged)

God's future plan

Then Boaz announced to the elders and all the people, 'Today you are witnesses that I have bought from Naomi all the property of Elimelek, Kilion and Mahlon. I have also acquired Ruth the Moabite, Mahlon's widow, as my wife...' So Boaz took Ruth and she became his wife. When he made love to her, the Lord enabled her to conceive, and she gave birth to a son... And they named him Obed... Obed the father of Jesse, and Jesse the father of David.

I love a happy ending. Although 'buying' a wife and talking about her as property is alien, we at last hear that Boaz is going to take Ruth to be his wife. This is a truly public declaration and nothing after this can take it away. All that hardship, waiting and trusting has finally reached a good and happy outcome for both Ruth and Naomi. We also find out that this is part of God's eternal plan. King David and ultimately Jesus himself become descendants of Ruth and Boaz through their son, Obed.

God had a plan for them right from the beginning. Following bereavement, we too can be sure that God has a future plan and purpose for us – both in our present lives and in eternity through Jesus, the alpha and omega, the beginning and the end. As the saying goes, 'Everything will be okay in the end. If it's not okay, it's not the end.'

■ PRAYER

Dear God, help us to keep trusting in your goodness through thick and thin until we know your purposes for our lives, both now and in our future with you. Amen

Always learning

Angela Tilby

'It is never too late' – how often do we hear that phrase? In the Christian life 'never too late' provides an important insight. While we are alive we are called to be disciples, students, learners in the school of Christ.

Whether your faith goes back to childhood, or whether it has been acquired more recently, there is always more to learn. God is infinite and he desires for us to share in the fruits of his Godhead, the final fulfilment which we call everlasting life.

These daily Bible readings are taken from different books of the Bible, from Genesis all the way through to one of the last books of the Bible, the letter to the Hebrews. All the selected verses encourage us to be active learners, to approach life, as far as we can, with the openness and expectation of a child. Getting old can be a burden, but it can also be a time of extraordinary grace, of greater dependency on God, of a lightness of being that can bring genuine hope to others. There is always something new to learn, just as there is always something to be thankful for.

Genesis 3:22–23 (NRSV)

Exiled from Eden

Then the Lord God said, 'See the man has become like one of us, knowing good and evil; and now, he might reach out his hand and take also from the tree of life, and eat, and live forever' – therefore the Lord God sent him forth from the garden of Eden, to till the ground from which he was taken.

We are not born perfect. One interpretation of the garden of Eden story is that the real sin of Adam and Eve was that they wanted to snatch at eternal life without going through the process of growing up. In this interpretation, the exile from Eden was more an act of mercy than of judgement, as God wants us to enjoy his new creation as mature sons and daughters. What do you think about this way of interpreting the story?

Like every toddler, we need to learn limits and boundaries. Our earthly life is sometimes described in the spiritual tradition as an exile, but it could also be seen as an education, a place to experiment and grow and bear fruit.

Much of this is hard and challenging, but we should always keep in mind that though our years on earth may be full of toil and disappointment, the end is glory. And this glory is being formed now, moment by moment, as we place our lives in God's hands and trust him with our everyday concerns.

■ PRAYER

Lord, by small steps, day by day, bring me closer to you. Amen

Proverbs 8:1–5 (NRSV)

The call of wisdom

Does not wisdom call, and does not understanding raise her voice? On the heights, beside the way, at the crossroads she takes her stand; beside the gates in front of the town, at the entrance of the portals she cries out: 'To you, O people, I call, and my cry is to all who live. O simple ones, learn prudence, acquire intelligence, you who lack it.'

In the Bible, wisdom is not the same thing as knowledge. The invitation to live wisely goes out to all of us, regardless of our educational status or achievements.

The Bible suggests that true wisdom begins with 'the fear of the Lord' (Proverbs 9:10). We grow into it by seeking God and living within the limits that God has set. We know from experience that selfishness and greed are deeply unattractive and put us instinctively on our guard. The clues and cues to a wise life are all around us; we just have to look.

Everywhere there are examples of lives lived generously and well. Such lives attract others and bear fruit, not because they are necessarily successful, but because they display cheerfulness, kindness, compassion and integrity.

■ PRAYER

O God, let me never despair of myself. Help me to see in others the kindness of your face, and to imitate those whose generosity and good humour make me smile. Amen

Psalm 119:33–38 (NRSV)

Walking in the way

Teach me, O Lord, the way of your statutes, and I will observe it to the end. Give me understanding, that I may keep your law and observe it with my whole heart. Lead me in the path of your commandments, for I delight in it. Turn my heart to your decrees, and not to selfish gain. Turn my eyes from looking at vanities; give me life in your ways. Confirm to your servant your promise, which is for those who fear you.

Every verse of this psalm refers to the ways in which God guides us to know his will. A range of different words are used: God's commandments, statutes, ordinances, precepts.

At the heart of them all is the concept of *Torah*, which we translate as 'law', but in Jewish and Hebrew tradition has a much wider meaning. *Torah* is like a beautiful, complex but ever accessible poem, inscribed in nature and in our hearts. It is not primarily intended to limit or restrict us, but to liberate us, enabling us to become what, in our deepest selves, we would most like to be.

The psalm is an illustration of *Torah*, a poem, a song of praise to the God of life. So sing! We are never too young to begin to understand the ways of God and never too old to stop seeking.

■ **PRAYER**
I will praise you, O God. From the depth of my being I will give thanks to you with all that I am. Amen

Isaiah 50:4–5, 7a (NRSV)

Listening and responding

The Lord God has given me the tongue of a teacher, that I may know how to sustain the weary with a word. Morning by morning he wakens – wakens my ear to listen as those who are taught. The Lord God has opened my ear, and I was not rebellious, I did not turn backwards... The Lord God helps me, therefore I have not been disgraced.

This is part of one of Isaiah's 'servant songs' which Christians have always interpreted as pointing to the life and death of Christ. The 'I' in these verses is, like Christ, obedient to God even to the point of suffering and self-sacrifice.

We will be most fruitful and fulfilled as believers if we make listening to God a priority – morning by morning. We cannot teach unless we are prepared to be taught, and perhaps the most important part of each day is the time we spend pondering the scriptures or merely waiting in God's presence.

Just as Christ was obedient to the Father, so we need to receive from God before we presume to speak for him. There are no shortcuts to living a fruitful and creative life.

■ PRAYER

Speak, Lord, for your servant is listening. When I wake and am still weary, sustain me with your word. Make me receptive, attentive and generous with my time as you have been generous with me in forgiving my sins and raising me to life with you. Amen

Luke 10:38–40a (NRSV)

At the Lord's feet

Now as they went on their way, [Jesus] entered a certain village, where a woman named Martha welcomed him into her home. She had a sister named Mary, who sat at the Lord's feet and listened to what he was saying. But Martha was distracted by her many tasks.

This little scene between Mary and Martha often makes us feel sorry for Martha. She was, after all, the busy one, always full of work to do, ticking off her household jobs. Mary, on the other hand, adopts the posture of a disciple, sitting attentively at Jesus' feet.

The contrast between the two sisters is real, but it should not be overdone. We cannot escape the tasks that life requires of us. But we can be more relaxed about them. We can be more purposeful, less driven. Distraction is inevitable in prayer, as in life, but we can learn to recentre ourselves, to imitate Mary even as, like Martha, we also welcome Jesus into our home and our life. And remember that Jesus loves both sisters, understanding their different temperaments and temptations.

■ **PRAYER**

Be present with us, Lord, in our daily tasks, and help us to keep focused on you. Teach us to be alert in your presence, encourage us when we are weary, protect us from all anxiety and help us to rest, trusting in your unfailing goodness. Amen

Matthew 5:2–6 (NRSV)

True blessing

Then [Jesus] began to speak, and taught them, saying, 'Blessed are the poor in spirit, for theirs is the kingdom of heaven. Blessed are those who mourn, for they will be comforted. Blessed are the meek, for they will inherit the earth. Blessed are those who hunger and thirst for righteousness, for they will be filled.'

We forget how contrary Jesus' teaching is to our expectations. These verses from the sermon on the mount are an assault on any idea that we can make our own luck or that right attitudes determine our fate in life.

Such ideas are very common today and they need to be challenged because they can make us complacent in the face of injustice. In God's economy we do not 'get what we deserve'; we do not create our own good fortune. Those who credit themselves for their successes in life are in reality woefully lacking.

The truth is that it is the vulnerable and the helpless who are most blessed by God. They are, without always knowing it, the agents of change, the heralds of a better future. It is their cries that bring God's kingdom near. This teaching is intended to shake us out of complacency, while consoling those who are beyond human consolation.

■ PRAYER

Blessed and holy God, when I have nothing to offer but tears and fears, unite them to your sufferings and bring your holy kingdom to birth in my heart. For I am nothing without you. Amen

Luke 9:1–3 (NRSV)

Learning the kingdom

Then Jesus called the twelve together and gave them power and authority over all demons and to cure diseases, and he sent them out to proclaim the kingdom of God and to heal. He said to them, 'Take nothing for your journey, no staff, nor bag, nor bread, nor money – not even an extra tunic.'

Following Jesus requires us to hold lightly to our own hopes, fears and ambitions. This does not come naturally to us. For most of us it is really hard not to put our own interests first. Yet living lightly to ourselves is part of learning to trust God day by day.

Jesus sent his disciples out with nothing because it was important that they experienced their own vulnerability. Given the challenges that lay ahead it was vital that they learned to trust in God, and not themselves, to make their mission fruitful.

There are times in our own lives, especially as we get older, when we can experience extreme vulnerability through illness, bereavement and loss. The teaching of Jesus suggests that even these times can be times when the kingdom breaks in and healing comes about in unexpected ways. Sometimes we just need to let it happen.

■ PRAYER

Lord, teach me that when I am most alone, I am still connected to you – even when I have nothing, I have everything in you. May your kingdom come and your will be done today. Amen

John 16:12–13 (NRSV)

The Spirit of truth

'I still have many things to say to you, but you cannot bear them now. When the Spirit of truth comes, he will guide you into all the truth; for he will not speak on his own, but will speak whatever he hears, and he will declare to you the things that are to come.'

Taxi drivers in London are qualified by 'doing the knowledge', proving that they can find their way through the complex maze of all London's streets. Christian knowledge, by contrast, can never be complete.

We can never have full knowledge because the wisdom of God is infinite, and we can only take in as much as our human nature can bear at any one time. Yet even as we recognise our limits, so we acknowledge that the journey into truth is never ending. Jesus leaves his disciples on the eve of his passion, but he promises them that he will be present with them through the Spirit.

The future is never closed because our relationship with God has no end. The Spirit of God is promised to all who believe and assures us that we are loved eternally and that the future is in his hands.

■ **PRAYER**

Come, Holy Spirit, bring me to life. When I am thirsty, refresh me;
when I am cold, kindle my heart; when I am tired, invigorate me.
Keep me safe under the shadow of your wings, today and all my days.
Amen

Romans 8:26–27 (NRSV)

Asking the Spirit to help

Likewise the Spirit helps us in our weakness; for we do not know how to pray as we ought, but that very Spirit intercedes with sighs too deep for words. And God, who searches the heart, knows what is the mind of the Spirit, because the Spirit intercedes for the saints according to the will of God.

One of the words used in John's gospel for the Holy Spirit is *paraclete*, a word usually translated as 'advocate'. But the Greek word *paraclete* is much richer than this rather dry legal term might suggest.

The Spirit is 'the Lord, the giver of life' as the Creed asserts. He is God's gift to us, and his presence helps us manage our burdens. The Spirit shares the weight and bears the load, always assuring us of God's love for us, and pointing us towards the fulfilment of God's promises.

So we can be assured that even when our prayers seem dry and meaningless, the Spirit is praying deep in us and is holding us within God's good purposes. The Spirit is also our teacher, reminding us of what we already know, unfolding to us new depths of God's truth and inspiring us to trust that our future is safe in God.

■ PRAYER

Come Spirit of truth, guide me into all truth. Come comforter, come advocate, come, kindle the flame of divine love within my heart, come and make me Christ's forever. Amen

Hebrews 10:23–25 (NRSV)

Learning together

Let us hold fast to the confession of our faith without wavering, for he who has promised is faithful. And let us consider how to provoke one another to love and good deeds, not neglecting to meet together, as is the habit of some, but encouraging one another, and all the more as you see the Day approaching.

It is often said that there is no such thing as a solitary Christian. We are meant to support one another and to learn from one another.

The Christian church is not a club for isolated individuals but a community of mutual learning and encouragement. As God is faithful to us, so we should be faithful to one another, even when we disagree or are divided by preferences and temperament. One of the greatest gifts we can give to one another is the gift of encouragement.

Young to old, old to young, across barriers of class, gender and race, an encouraging word makes a huge difference. Try it today, because 'the Day', the day of God's fulfilment, is always approaching.

■ PRAYER

Teach me, good Lord, to serve you with courage and goodwill. To curb my grumbles, to see the good in those around me, to forgive those who misunderstand me and always to look to you, my Saviour and my God. Amen

Planning for the future

For I know the plans I have for you, declares the Lord, plans for welfare and not for evil, to give you a future and a hope.
JEREMIAH 29:11 (ESV)

Change is inevitable, and in recent years the idea of the unexpected has become so familiar one might even say that it is expected! In times of turmoil and uncertainty, these words bring comfort. Where our plans may seem like a mess, God has a plan for us – one that promises hope. Jeremiah's words were written to Jewish people who had been forced to settle in a foreign country – they may have desired a quick fix, a promise of immediate safety and security. Instead, God promises that he has a plan, that he will give them a future and a hope.

Making plans for the long term can be intimidating, especially when thinking about the future and providing for our loved ones. But we can make those plans in the knowledge that God knows what lies ahead and is here for us in the present to show us into a hopeful future.

One important way to plan for the future is to make a will. Many find this to be an anxious or complicated process, but it doesn't need to be. At BRF, we are reliant on fundraising activities, donations and gifts in wills to enable us to do our work. We are hugely grateful to everyone who remembers BRF in their will or who makes a donation in memory of a loved one. After you have made provision for your family, friends and church, would you kindly consider a gift of 1% in your will to help BRF? We always recommend visiting a solicitor to ensure that your will accurately represents your wishes. All you need to take to your solicitor is our registered charity number, which is 233280.

For more information on making a gift to BRF in your will please contact our fundraising team on **01235 462305** or via **giving@brf.org.uk**.

We thank you for your support and your prayers.

The BRF fundraising team

In this year's BRF Advent book Sally Welch explores two questions: What is the Christmas story really about, and how do we share it? Through each week of Advent, a different aspect of the Christmas story is examined: light, promise, mystery, love, peace and hope. Within each week, the days are focused on the ways in which the Christmas story is shared: prophecies, journeys, new life, signs, poems, stories and conversations. Each day offers a Bible passage, followed by a reflection and prayer activity. Suggestions for group study and group study questions are also included.

Sharing the Christmas Story
From reading to living the gospel
Sally Welch
978 1 80039 106 3 £8.99
brfonline.org.uk

BIBLE REFLECTIONS FOR OLDER PEOPLE **GROUP SUBSCRIPTION FORM**

All our Bible reading notes can be ordered online
by visiting **brfonline.org.uk/subscriptions**

The group subscription rate for *Bible Reflections for Older People* will be £16.05 per person until April 2023.

☐ I would like to take out a group subscription for .... (*quantity*) copies.

☐ Please start my order with the January 2023 / May 2023 / September 2023* issue.
   (*delete as appropriate*)

Please do not send any money with your order. Send your order to BRF and we will send you an invoice.

Name and address of the person organising the group subscription:

Title .... First name/initials .... Surname ....

Address ....

.... Postcode ....

Telephone .... Email ....

Church ....

Name and address of the person paying the invoice if the invoice needs to be sent directly to them:

Title .... First name/initials .... Surname ....

Address ....

.... Postcode ....

Telephone .... Email ....

Please return this form to:
BRF, 15 The Chambers, Vineyard, Abingdon OX14 3FE | **enquiries@brf.org.uk**
For terms and cancellation information, please visit **brfonline.org.uk/terms**.

Bible Reading Fellowship is a charity (233280) and company limited by guarantee (301324),
registered in England and Wales

BIBLE REFLECTIONS FOR OLDER PEOPLE INDIVIDUAL/GIFT SUBSCRIPTION FORM

> To order online, please visit **brfonline.org.uk/subscriptions**

☐ I would like to take out a subscription (*complete your name and address details only once*)
☐ I would like to give a gift subscription (*please provide both names and addresses*)

Title .... First name/initials .... Surname..

Address...

.... Postcode ....

Telephone .... Email ....

Gift subscription name ....

Gift subscription address ....

.... Postcode ....

Gift message (*20 words max. or include your own gift card*):

....

....

Please send *Bible Reflections for Older People* beginning with the January 2023 / May 2023 / September 2023* issue (**delete as appropriate*):

(*please tick box*)	**UK**	**Europe**	**Rest of world**
Bible Reflections for Older People	☐ £20.25	☐ £27.75	☐ £31.80

Total enclosed £ .... (*cheques should be made payable to 'BRF'*)

Please charge my MasterCard / Visa with £ ....

Card no. ☐☐☐☐ ☐☐☐☐ ☐☐☐☐ ☐☐☐☐

Expires end ☐☐ ☐☐ Security code ☐☐☐ Last 3 digits on the reverse of the card

We will use your personal data to process this order. From time to time we may send you information about the work of BRF. Please contact us if you wish to discuss your mailing preferences **brf.org.uk/privacy**

Please return this form to:
BRF, 15 The Chambers, Vineyard, Abingdon OX14 3FE | **enquiries@brf.org.uk**
For terms and cancellation information, please visit **brfonline.org.uk/terms**.

Bible Reading Fellowship is a charity (233280) and company limited by guarantee (301324), registered in England and Wales